Green Princess COOKBOOK

Barbara Beery

Photography by Zac Williams

GIBBS SMITH
TO ENRICH AND INSPIRE HUMANKIND

Salt Lake City | Charleston | Santa Fe | Santa Barbara

First Edition
13 12 11 10 09   20 19 18 17 16 15 14 13 12 11 10 9 8 7 6 5 4 3 2 1
Text © 2009 Barbara Beery
Photographs © 2009 Zac Williams

Published by
Gibbs Smith
P.O. Box 667
Layton, Utah 84041

Orders: 1.800.835.4993
www.gibbs-smith.com
www.batterupkids.com
www.kidscookingshop.com

Designed by m:GraphicDesign / Maralee Nelson
Printed and bound in China

Gibbs Smith books are printed on either recycled, 100% post consumer waste, or FSC-certified papers.

Library of Congress Cataloging-in-Publication Data

Beery, Barbara, 1954-
   Green Princess cookbook / Barbara Beery ; photographs by Zac Williams. — 1st ed.
      p. cm.
   ISBN-13: 978-1-4236-0565-2
   ISBN-10: 1-4236-0565-9
   1. Cookery (Natural foods)—Juvenile literature. I. Williams, Zac, ill. II. Title.
   TX741.B43 2009
   641.5'636—dc22
                                    2008038192

Contents
· · · · · · · · · ·

It's Easy Being Green!

What's Organic?

Organic food is grown by farmers who use only natural ingredients—no chemical pesticides or fertilizers that are harmful to the planet. You can buy organic fruit, vegetables, milk, eggs, and other things. Organic food tastes better too!

Buying Local

When you buy locally, your food is not shipped from far away. This helps save gas and keeps our air and water cleaner. Local food is also fresher, because it's picked ripe in season. And buying locally helps support the farmers in your neighborhood too.

100-Mile Diet

Try to buy fruits and veggies that are grown within 100 miles of where you live. It's better for the planet than buying food that has traveled to your table by ship or plane an average of 1,500 miles!

Farm-to-Table

Farm-to-Table is a nonprofit organization that helps strengthen ties between local farmers and local communities.

Farmers Markets

Farmers markets are a great place to go with your family to buy organic and locally grown food. Look for a farmers market near you because farmers markets are often set up in a park or parking lot and meet once or twice a week. It's a fun way to shop!

Community Supported Agriculture

Community Supported Agriculture, or CSA for short, is a group made up of families or other groups that promise to support local farms. If you are part of a CSA, you get to share fruits and veggies grown by local farmers.

Community Gardens

A community garden is a special garden where a group of people decide to share the land, the work of growing the garden, and best of all, the delicious foods that you grow!

Grass-Fed Meats

When you buy beef that was grass-fed, it is better for the cows, the farmers, and the planet.

Vegetable-Based Food Dyes

You can get food colorings and dyes made from natural ingredients, like beets or berries or spices. You can also get colorful sprinkles, sanding sugars, and other decorating candies made with natural dyes.

• • • • • • • • • • •

All recipes in this book should be made using organic and local ingredients whenever possible.

Solar-Power Strawberry Lemonade

Ingredients

• • • • • • • •

1½ cups unrefined sugar

1 cup chopped organic strawberries

2 strips organic lemon zest

2 cups water

2 cups freshly squeezed organic lemon juice

¼ teaspoon vanilla

2 to 3 cups water, chilled

Garnish

Organic lemon slices, strawberry slices, and mint

Serves 6–8

Place sugar, strawberries, lemon zest, and water in a half-gallon container with a lid.

Stir ingredients to blend (sugar will not be totally dissolved) and secure lid. Shake container four to five times to continue mixing.

Place container in full sun (on a sunny windowsill or outside) for 1 hour. After an hour, shake again a few times and return to a sunny spot for another 30 minutes.

Pour the strawberry sugar syrup through a strainer over a large bowl or pitcher.

Add the lemon juice, vanilla, and 2 cups chilled water. Stir and then taste; add more water or sugar as desired.

Serve immediately over ice or store, covered, in the refrigerator and serve later the same day.

Green Living Tip

You can save gas or electricity by using sunlight to heat water! What about other ideas for solar power? Try hanging your laundry outside to air dry instead of using the dryer or buying a little solar light for your yard that charges up in the day and gives off light at night.

Soy-to-the-World Smoothies

Ingredients

• • • • • • • •

1 organic banana, sliced

½ cup organic sliced strawberries

½ cup organic raspberries

½ cup organic cherries, pitted

1 cup vanilla soy milk

½ cup vanilla soy yogurt

½ teaspoon vanilla

Additional diced organic fruit for garnish (optional)

Serves 2

Place all ingredients in a blender and process until smooth and creamy.

Serve with an extra sprinkling of fresh fruit on top, if desired.

Green Living Tip

Soy protein is a great way to get protein without eating meat. Cattle and beef production are hard on the environment, so getting protein from other sources can make your body strong and help the earth too!

Slurp 'n' Slushy Organic Berry Cooler

Ingredients

• • • • • • • •

½ cup freshly squeezed organic orange juice

1 cup whole-fruit raspberry sorbet

¼ cup fresh or frozen organic cranberries

¼ cup sliced fresh or frozen organic strawberries

Crushed ice

Serves 2

Combine orange juice, raspberry sorbet, cranberries, and strawberries in a blender.

Blend until smooth and serve over crushed ice.

Green Cuisine Tip

For the freshest berries, go to farmers' markets that offer berries harvested that same day. Some berry farms even allow you to pick your own berries . . . and that would be a "berry" good time!

Sunshine Sorbet

Ingredients

- ¾ cup water
- ¾ cup unrefined sugar
- 1 teaspoon grated fresh ginger
- 2 cups freshly squeezed organic orange juice
- 1 organic lemon, juiced
- 1 cup coconut milk
- 2½ cups peeled and chopped fresh organic mango

Garnish

  Seasonal organic fresh fruit

Serves 6–8

Heat water, sugar, and ginger in a small saucepan until sugar dissolves completely. Set aside, covered, for about 1 hour to cool completely.

When cooled, combine sugar mixture (called simple syrup) with remaining ingredients in a blender and puree until smooth.

Pour into the container of an ice cream maker and freeze according to manufacturer's instructions.

Store in the freezer in an airtight container for up to 3 days. Remove from freezer 5 to 10 minutes before serving. Garnish with plenty of fresh fruit.

Green Cuisine Tip

Instead of serving it in a bowl, serve Sunshine Sorbet in hollowed-out orange, lemon, or lime halves. Then save those rinds to compost in your garden!

Jungle Boogie Banana Ice Cream

Ingredients
● ● ● ● ● ● ●

5 to 6 ripe organic bananas

1 tablespoon freshly squeezed organic orange juice

¾ cup honey or molasses

1 tablespoon vanilla

1½ cups heavy cream

Garnish

1 cup chocolate syrup

1 cup shredded coconut, toasted

1 cup sliced fresh organic strawberries

Makes 1 quart

Slice bananas and place on a sheet pan. Place in freezer for 1 hour before using.

Place frozen banana slices and orange juice in a blender. Process for 10 to 15 seconds. Add honey or molasses and vanilla and process again.

While the blender is running, slowly pour in the heavy cream and blend until smooth. Chill mixture covered in refrigerator for 1 hour.

Transfer mixture to an ice cream maker and process according to the manufacturer's instructions. When ice cream is finished, place in an airtight container and freeze for several hours before serving. Remove from freezer 5 to 10 minutes before serving and garnish with chocolate syrup, coconut, and strawberries.

Green Cuisine Tip

Always buy organic bananas! Bananas are a great energy booster and a good source of vitamins and minerals.

Cheery Chocolate Dip

Ingredients

- 1 cup heavy cream
- 2 cups chopped semisweet or milk chocolate
- 1 tablespoon freshly grated ginger
- 1 teaspoon vanilla

Makes 3 cups

In a medium saucepan, heat the cream over medium-low heat for 2 to 3 minutes. When cream is hot, gradually add the chocolate, stirring until melted and smooth. Stir in ginger and cook 1 minute more.

Remove from heat and add vanilla, stirring to blend. Transfer to a bowl and serve with fresh fruit dippers or gingersnaps.

Earth-Friendly Edamame Dip

Ingredients

- ½ cup frozen edamame, cooked, cooled, and shelled
- ½ cup vegetable broth
- ¼ cup chopped organic red onion
- 3 tablespoons chopped fresh organic cilantro or parsley
- 2 tablespoons rice vinegar
- 1 tablespoon extra virgin olive oil
- ½ teaspoon sea salt
- 1½ teaspoons Asian chili garlic sauce
- 1 can (16 ounces) white beans, drained and rinsed

Makes about 2½ cups

Place all ingredients in a food processor and process about 45 seconds or until smooth and creamy.

Serve immediately with Handmade Fiesta Tortillas (page 39) or fresh veggie dippers. Dip can be covered and chilled in the refrigerator for up to 3 days.

Organic Orchard Salsa

Ingredients

- 2 organic apples (any type), peeled and cut into chunks
- 5 organic apricots, pitted and cut into chunks
- 2 organic plums, peeled, pitted, and cut into chunks
- 3 tablespoons honey
- ½ teaspoon vanilla

Serves 4-6

Place apples, apricots, plums, and honey in a saucepan.

Cover and cook over medium heat for 15 minutes. Mixture should simmer but not boil.

Remove from heat, add vanilla, and cool 10 minutes. Crush fruits lightly with a potato masher or fork.

Serve immediately with Cinnamon-Maple Crisps (page 20) or with yogurt and granola. It also makes a great topping for ice cream or frozen yogurt. You can store in a covered container in the refrigerator for up to 1 week.

Green Cuisine Tip

Organic food is grown, raised, or manufactured by farmers using only natural ingredients. A product can be labeled "organic," only after the farm where the food is grown is inspected to make sure the farmer is following all the rules necessary to meet USDA organic standards. The next time you are in the grocery store, look for the certified USDA organic label.

Cinnamon-Maple Crisps

Ingredients

- 24 (3½-inch) wonton wrappers
- 2 teaspoons maple syrup or honey
- ½ teaspoon ground cinnamon

Makes about 24

Preheat oven to 375 degrees F. Line 2 sheet pans with Silpat, unbleached parchment paper, or a clean brown paper grocery bag cut to fit pans. Set aside.

In a small bowl, combine maple syrup or honey and cinnamon.

Carefully remove wonton wrappers from package, one at a time, and place on a cutting board. Using assorted 2-inch cookie cutters, cut wonton wrappers into various shapes. Place cutouts ½ inch apart on prepared sheet pans.

Lightly brush each wrapper with cinnamon-honey mixture.

Place sheet pans in oven and bake for about 4 to 6 minutes. Watch the crackers carefully as they brown fast!

Remove from oven and cool for 5 minutes before removing crackers from pan and serving. Serve with Organic Orchard Salsa (page 19) or Cheery Chocolate Dip (page 16).

Vine-Fresh Veggie Queso

Ingredients

- - - - - - - -

1 tablespoon unsalted butter

1 tablespoon unbleached flour

2 cups heavy cream

1 cup grated Monterey Jack cheese

½ cup grated mild cheddar cheese

¼ teaspoon sea salt

1 organic tomato, diced

1 organic jalapeño or serrano chile pepper, diced

½ cup diced organic red bell pepper

½ cup fresh organic corn, cut from the cob

1 cup coarsely chopped organic zucchini or broccoli

Serves 6-8

In a medium saucepan over low heat, add butter and slowly melt. Stir in flour until mixture is free of lumps.

Add cream and whisk to combine. Stirring constantly, heat up until mixture thickens, about 5 minutes. Add cheese and whisk vigorously until completely melted.

Stir in salt, tomato, peppers, corn, and zucchini or broccoli. Cook for 1 minute and transfer to a serving dish.

Serve warm with seasonal veggie dippers or tortilla chips.

Green Cuisine Tip

Eat fresh veggies in season. You can add different veggies or leave out others depending on what's growing when you make your dip.

Dig-That-Earth-Day Hummus

Ingredients

• • • • • • • •

2 cups canned chickpeas, drained and rinsed

2 to 3 medium-size cooked organic beets, coarsely chopped

2 cloves garlic, peeled

3 tablespoons organic lemon juice

¼ cup water

3 tablespoons tahini

½ teaspoon ground cumin

½ teaspoon paprika

Garnish

1 teaspoon extra virgin olive oil

1 tablespoon minced organic flat-leaf parsley

Makes about 2 cups

Place chickpeas and beets in a food processor along with the garlic, lemon juice, and water; process about 1 minute. Add more water if needed to form a smooth and creamy consistency.

Add tahini, cumin, and paprika and blend another 30 seconds to combine.

Serve immediately or store covered in the refrigerator up to 3 days. To serve, place in a shallow dish and garnish with a drizzle of olive oil and minced parsley. Serve with plenty of whole grain bread or pita bread.

Green Living Tip

Connect to nature and grow your own garden! The tastiest and freshest veggies are the ones you grow in your very own backyard. If you live in a large city, grow fruits, veggies, or herbs in pots or window boxes.

Community Garden Soup Pots

Ingredients
● ● ● ● ● ● ●

2 tablespoons extra virgin olive oil

1 cup chopped organic green onions

½ teaspoon sea salt

1 cup sliced organic carrots (peeled and cut into rounds)

1 cup organic potatoes, cut into large cubes

1 cup organic green beans

1 quart chicken or vegetable broth

2 cups chopped organic tomatoes

½ teaspoon freshly ground black pepper

½ cup frozen peas

1 cup cubed cheese

Serves 6

Heat olive oil in large pot over medium-low heat for 1 minute.

Add the onions and salt. Cook, stirring occasionally, for about 5 minutes. Add the carrots, potatoes, and beans and cook 4 to 5 minutes more, stirring occasionally.

Add the broth, tomatoes, and pepper. Increase heat and bring to a simmer; then lower heat, cover, and cook about 30 minutes or until all veggies are fork-tender.

Remove pot from heat and stir in frozen peas.

Carefully ladle soup into bowls or mugs. Top with a few cubes of cheese.

Green Living Tip

Join a community garden. It's a way for neighbors and friends to share a garden plot, the work of planting, weeding, and watering—and the harvest!

Nature's Veggie Nachos

Ingredients

- 1 medium organic sweet potato, peeled and sliced into thin rounds
- 1 tablespoon canola oil
- ½ teaspoon sea salt
- ½ teaspoon paprika
- ½ teaspoon ground cumin
- ½ cup grated Monterey Jack cheese
- ⅓ cup chopped organic tomatoes
- ⅓ cup chopped organic bell peppers
- ⅓ cup chopped organic green onions
- 1 organic serrano or jalapeño pepper, chopped (optional)

Garnish

- ¼ cup sour cream
- 1 tablespoon chopped organic cilantro

Serves 4

Preheat the oven to 450 degrees F. Line a sheet pan with Silpat, unbleached parchment paper, or a clean brown paper grocery bag cut to fit. Spray with nonstick cooking spray and set aside.

Place cut potatoes on prepared sheet pan. Pour oil evenly over the potatoes and sprinkle with salt, paprika, and cumin. Toss with your hands to coat all sides.

Arrange potatoes in a single layer on prepared pan and bake for 25 minutes, or until the rounds are almost tender.

Remove from oven and top with cheese and chopped veggies. Return to oven and bake for 5 to 7 minutes, or until cheese has melted. Remove from oven, garnish, and serve immediately.

Eggs-actly Frittatas

Ingredients

8 eggs

½ cup whole milk

½ teaspoon freshly ground black pepper

¼ teaspoon sea salt

4 ounces thinly sliced turkey or ham, chopped

⅓ cup freshly grated Parmesan

1 tablespoon chopped fresh organic flat-leaf parsley

2 cups chopped organic red bell pepper

Makes 12

Preheat the oven to 375 degrees F. Spray two 12-cup muffin pans with nonstick cooking spray.

Whisk together eggs, milk, pepper, and salt in a large bowl. Stir in turkey or ham, cheese, and parsley.

Fill prepared muffin cups almost to the top with the egg mixture. Sprinkle with chopped bell pepper. Bake until the egg mixture puffs and is just set in the center, about 8 to 10 minutes. Using a rubber spatula, loosen the frittatas from the muffin cups and slide onto a platter. Serve immediately.

Green Living Tip

Keep these tips in mind for clean and green dishwashing:
- If you only have a few dishes, use a sink full of water instead of the dishwater.
- Use eco-friendly dish soap.
- Use leftover dishwater to water houseplants.
- If you use the dishwasher, turn off the heated drying cycle and open the dishwasher door to let the dishes air dry.

So-Good Soba Noodle Nests

Ingredients

- - - - - - - -

- 1 package (8 ounces) soba noodles
- 1 tablespoon canola oil
- 2 cups thinly sliced organic red bell pepper
- ¼ cup minced fresh ginger
- 1 clove garlic, minced
- 3 cups sliced assorted organic summer squash
- 3 tablespoons tamari
- 1½ cups chicken or vegetable broth
- 2 teaspoons rice vinegar
- 2 cups organic snow peas
- ½ cup shredded organic carrots
- 1 tablespoon minced organic cilantro
- 2 organic green onions, thinly sliced
- 2 tablespoons dark sesame oil

Serves 4–6

Prepare soba noodles according to package directions. Drain, cover, and keep warm in a pot.

Heat canola oil in a large nonstick skillet over medium-high heat. Toss in pepper, ginger, and garlic. Cook for 2 minutes.

Stir in squash, tamari, broth, and rice vinegar. Saute 3 minutes and toss in snow peas, carrots, cilantro, and onions. Cook another 2 to 3 minutes. Toss with sesame oil.

Scoop the warm noodles equally onto plates in small round nests and top with stir-fried vegetables. This dish is good served warm or at room temperature.

Off-the-Vine Zany Zucchini Muffins

Ingredients

1 package spice cake mix

4 eggs

⅔ cup canola oil

1 teaspoon ground cinnamon

2 cups grated organic zucchini, unpeeled

Makes 24

Preheat oven to 350 degrees F. In a large bowl combine the cake mix, eggs, canola oil, and cinnamon. Stir in zucchini until incorporated into batter.

Using an ice-cream scoop, scoop batter into 24 unbleached paper or silicone muffin cups, filling the cups two-thirds full.

Bake for 20 minutes or until toothpick inserted in a muffin's center comes out clean.

Remove from oven and let cool in pans for 10 minutes. Remove from pans. Serve immediately or cool and store covered for up to 2 days.

Green Living Tip

You can become an energy-saving baker by doing the following:
- Keeping the oven door shut while baking. No peeking!
- Using your inside oven light to look through the oven door window to check your dish.
- Not preheating the oven to warm up leftover food.
- Baking smaller items in a toaster oven.

Cornbread in a Recycled Can

Ingredients

- 10 to 12 empty cans (8 to 14 ounces each), tops and labels removed, washed and dried
- Parchment paper
- 1 cup stone-ground cornmeal, plus more for cans
- 1 cup unbleached flour
- ⅔ cup unrefined sugar
- ½ teaspoon sea salt
- 3 teaspoons baking powder
- 1 egg
- 1 cup plain soy milk
- ⅓ cup canola oil

Makes 10-12

Preheat oven to 400 degrees F. Line each can with parchment paper. Generously spray the parchment paper with nonstick cooking spray and sprinkle about ¼ teaspoon cornmeal inside each to coat the bottom and lower portion of the sides of each can. Place cans on a sheet pan and set aside.

In a large bowl, combine cornmeal, flour, sugar, salt, and baking powder with a whisk.

Stir in egg, soy milk, and oil until well combined.

Pour batter into prepared cans, filling three-fourths full. Bake in preheated oven for 15 to 20 minutes, or until a toothpick inserted into the center comes out clean.

Remove from oven and cool on a wire rack for 5 minutes. Serve in cans or remove before serving. Serve with Hooray for Homemade Butter (page 40) and honey.

Handmade Fiesta Tortillas

Ingredients
● ● ● ● ● ● ●

1 cup stone-ground whole
  wheat flour
1 cup unbleached flour
  plus ¼ cup for dusting
  work area
1 teaspoon baking powder
1 teaspoon sea salt
¼ cup canola oil
⅔ cup water

Makes 8

Combine flours, baking powder, and salt. Stir in the oil and water all at once, using a mixer or fork, and toss quickly.

When dough can be gathered into a soft ball, turn out onto a floured work area and knead several times.

Divide dough into 8 balls and cover with a light dusting of flour. Place on a sheet pan that has been sprayed with nonstick cooking spray and cover with a damp kitchen towel; let rest for 15 minutes.

Flatten first ball of dough into a disk. You can do this by either rolling out dough with a rolling pin on a floured surface to form into a 6-inch circle, or by flattening each disk in a tortilla press between two sheets of waxed paper. Repeat with remaining balls of dough.

Place each tortilla in an ungreased skillet that has been preheated to medium-high heat. Cook 30 seconds on each side until the tortilla has toasted brown spots. Stack tortillas on a plate as they are cooked and cover them with a dry kitchen towel.

Serve immediately with Hooray for Homemade Butter (page 40), Vine-Fresh Veggie Queso (page 23), or Earth-Friendly Edamame Dip (page 17). You can also use the tortillas to make quesadillas.

Hooray for Homemade Butter

Ingredients
● ● ● ● ● ● ● ●

- 2 cups heavy whipping cream
- 2 pint-size Mason jars, chilled
- 2 marbles, washed and chilled in freezer for 30 minutes
- 1/8 teaspoon sea salt

Makes about 1 cup

Divide cream evenly between 2 chilled jars and drop a chilled marble into each jar. Secure lid and start shaking.

At first you will hear the marble moving, but after about 5 to 10 minutes, the cream will be so thick that you won't hear or feel the marble. The sides of the jar will also become coated with thick cream.

Keep shaking for another 5 to 10 minutes. While you are shaking the jar, you will begin to hear the marble again and see the cream on the sides of the jar begin to disappear. During this time the butter will be forming.

All of a sudden you will see small lumps of butter with a milky liquid in the jar. Your butter is ready! Remove lid and pour butter and liquid into a strainer over a medium-sized bowl. Rinse the butter with cold water and let it sit in the strainer for 5 minutes. Remove strainer with butter and discard liquid in bowl.

With a paper towel, carefully pat butter dry to remove any drops of water. Place butter in small container and stir in salt. Store covered in refrigerator. Serve with Off-the-Vine Zany Zucchini Muffins (page 35) or any of your favorite breads.

Fresh-from-the-Vine Very Berry Jam

Ingredients
• • • • • • • •

1 cup each fresh organic raspberries, blackberries, strawberries, and blueberries

3 to 3½ cups unrefined sugar

⅛ teaspoon sea salt

2 tablespoons organic lemon juice

2 pint-size jam jars

Makes 2 pint-sized jars

Place berries in a large mixing bowl, sprinkle with sugar, and mash with a potato masher.

Pour mashed berries into a medium saucepan and cook over medium-low heat until juices are released.

Increase heat to high and bring to a boil. Stir occasionally and boil about 15 minutes until mixture begins to thicken. Lower heat and simmer for 5 minutes.

Remove from heat and stir in salt and lemon juice. Let cool for 10 minutes. Ladle jam into jars and seal with lids. Cool for 1 hour before placing in the refrigerator. May be kept refrigerated for up to 2 weeks.

Green Cuisine Tip

When it comes to choosing sugar, there is no doubt that unrefined sugar is the best choice. It contains minerals and nutrients that are stripped from refined white sugar and regular brown sugar when they are processed.

Nutty about Nut Butters

Ingredients

- 1 cup unsalted roasted peanuts, almonds, cashews, or macadamia nuts
- ¼ teaspoon sea salt
- 1 to 2 tablespoons vegetable oil
- Sugar to taste (optional)
- ¼ teaspoon cinnamon (optional)
- ¼ cup unsalted roasted chopped nuts for chunky butters (optional)

Makes about 1 cup

Place the nuts and salt in a food processor or blender and process until finely ground.

Add oil and continue processing until the nut butter becomes smooth and creamy, adding more oil if necessary. Add sugar and cinnamon, if using, and process to blend.

For chunky butters, stir chopped nuts into processed nut butter. Store in an airtight container, covered, in refrigerator for up to 2 weeks. Serve on crackers or whole grain bread with honey or Fresh-from-the-Vine Very Berry Jam (page 43). Nut butters are great in smoothies too!

Green Cuisine Tip

Unrefined natural sea salt is a better source of nutrients than mined rock salt. It is much higher in essential minerals because it has been living in the ocean for millions of years!

Fancy Frozen Flowerpots

Ingredients

• • • • • • • •

- 4 (2 to 3-inch) clay flowerpots
- 4 large marshmallows or 4 small pieces of cake
- 1 pint frozen yogurt
- 4 to 6 chocolate wafer cookies, crushed
- 4 Flower Power Cookies (page 50)

Makes 4 servings

Place a marshmallow or small piece of cake in the bottom of each clay pot. Press down, making sure to cover hole in the bottom of each pot.

Scoop frozen yogurt into each pot. Sprinkle evenly with crushed cookies.

Insert a Flower Power Cookie into the center of each flowerpot; serve immediately. Or you can prepare flowerpots with frozen yogurt ahead of time, cover, and freeze, and then remove and insert cookie just before serving.

Baby Butterfly Cupcakes

Ingredients

● ● ● ● ● ● ● ●

1 package vanilla or chocolate cake mix

Milk

3 cups powdered sugar

1 cup butter, cut into small chunks

1 teaspoon vanilla

1 to 2 tablespoons heavy whipping cream

Assorted food coloring

48 small pretzel twists or yogurt-covered pretzel twists

24 candy-coated chocolate candies

Assorted small jelly beans

Rope licorice, cut into ½-inch sections

Decorating sugars

Makes 24 cupcakes

Preheat oven to 350 degrees F. Line cupcake pans with silicone baking cups or paper baking cups. Set aside.

In a large mixing bowl, make cupcakes according to package directions, substituting milk for water.

Bake according to package directions. Cool for 30 minutes before frosting and decorating.

In a large bowl, mix together powdered sugar and butter. With an electric mixer, beat on low speed until well blended. Increase speed to medium and beat about 2 minutes.

Add vanilla, 1 tablespoon cream, and a small amount of food coloring. Beat on medium speed for 1 minute, adding more cream if needed for spreading consistency.

Frost each cupcake equally with frosting. Place a small candy-coated chocolate candy in the center top portion of a cupcake to form the head of the butterfly. Line up 3 to 5 jellybeans below the chocolate candy piece to form the body.

Insert a small pretzel twist at an angle on each side of the butterfly's body to make the wings and so it looks like the butterfly is flying. Insert 2 licorice strips into the cupcake above the candy-coated chocolate to make the butterfly's antennae.

Repeat for all cupcakes. Lightly sprinkle each with decorating sugars and serve.

Flower Power Cookies

Ingredients
● ● ● ● ● ● ● ●

Cookies

- ¾ cup butter, softened
- ½ cup brown sugar, packed
- 1 egg
- ¾ cup molasses
- 3 cups unbleached flour
- ¼ teaspoon sea salt
- 2 teaspoons ground ginger
- 1 teaspoon ground cinnamon
- ½ teaspoon ground cloves
- ½ teaspoon nutmeg
- Powdered sugar for rolling out dough
- Assorted candies
- Decorating sprinkles

Makes 12–14 cookies

Preheat oven to 350 degrees F. Line 2 cookie sheets with Silpat, unbleached parchment paper, or a clean brown paper grocery bag cut to fit.

In a large bowl, combine butter, brown sugar, egg, and molasses.

Stir in dry ingredients and mix completely. Cover bowl and put in refrigerator for 2 to 3 hours.

Take out small portions of the cookie dough (leave the rest covered in the fridge) and roll out on work area dusted with powdered sugar to ½-inch thickness. Cut out with a 2-inch flower-shaped cookie cutter. Place each cookie 2 inches apart on prepared cookie sheet and insert a lollipop stick into the bottom portion of each flower.

Bake for 12 to 14 minutes or until slightly browned. Remove cookies from oven and cool on cookie sheet on a wire rack for 10 minutes.

Frosting

- 3 tablespoons meringue powder
- 2 cups powdered sugar
- ¼ cup plus 2 tablespoons warm water
- 1 teaspoon vanilla
- ½ teaspoon almond extract
- Food coloring

Combine meringue powder, powdered sugar, water, vanilla, and almond extract in a mixing bowl.

Beat on high speed with an electric mixer for 3 to 5 minutes

Divide into separate bowls and add drops of food coloring as desired. Decorate cookies.

Power-Up Fruit Cup

Ingredients
● ● ● ● ● ● ●

1 cup assorted seasonal organic berries

1 cup sliced organic apples or pears

1 organic banana, peeled and sliced

1 organic mango, peeled and sliced

¼ cup assorted organic dried fruits such as raisins, cranberries, or cherries

1 to 2 tablespoons honey

4 to 6 tablespoons vanilla yogurt

4 to 6 tablespoons granola

Makes 4-6

Place fresh and dried fruit in a large mixing bowl, add honey, and gently toss.

Scoop equal amounts of fruit mixture into serving cups, drizzle with yogurt, and sprinkle with granola.

Green Cuisine Tip

In the summer growing season, fruits and vegetables are the most plentiful and taste the best! Learn how to can, freeze, dry, and dehydrate all of the sensational summer crops. That way you'll be sure to have plenty of the very freshest fruits and veggies all year long.

Back-to-Nature Fruit-Filled Meringues

Ingredients
● ● ● ● ● ● ● ●

- 3 egg whites, room temperature
- ¾ cup unrefined sugar
- ¼ teaspoon cream of tartar
- ¼ teaspoon vanilla or almond extract
- ¼ cup confetti sprinkles

Toppings
- 3 cups sliced or chopped assorted seasonal organic fresh fruit
- Whipped cream
- 3 tablespoons confetti sprinkles

Makes 18–24

Preheat oven to 250 degrees F. Line two sheet pans with Silpat, unbleached parchment paper, or a clean brown paper grocery bag cut to fit.

In a large bowl, whip egg whites with an electric mixer until soft peaks form. With mixer on, slowly add sugar, a tablespoon at a time. Add cream of tartar and vanilla or almond extract. Continue beating until stiff peaks form. Fold in ¼ cup sprinkles.

Spoon about 2 tablespoons of meringue into mounds on prepared sheet pans about ½ inch apart. With the back of the spoon, press in the center of each mound to form a small indention. This makes a nice little place to spoon on fruit later.

Place pans on middle rack of preheated oven. Bake for 1 hour. Turn off oven and leave door closed for 10 minutes. Remove pans from oven and remove meringues from baking sheets. Store in an airtight container until ready to use.

To serve, fill indentions with fruit and top with whipped cream and a few more sprinkles.

Green Cuisine Tip

Use candy sprinkles and food coloring made from natural vegetable dyes.

Chocolate Cobbler Cups

Ingredients

• • • • • • • •

⅓ cup unbleached flour

¼ cup cocoa powder

⅓ cup unrefined sugar

3 eggs

1 cup heavy cream

1 teaspoon vanilla

¼ teaspoon almond extract

1 cup chocolate chips

½ cup organic raspberries

¼ cup organic blueberries

Powdered sugar

Makes 4

Preheat oven to 350 degrees F. Spray nonstick cooking spray inside four oven-proof mugs or small coffee cups, place on a sheet pan, and set aside.

Combine flour, cocoa, and sugar in a large bowl. Whisk to combine ingredients.

In a smaller bowl, whisk together eggs, cream, vanilla, and almond extract. Add to dry mixture and stir until all ingredients are well combined.

With a mixing spoon, gently fold in chocolate chips, raspberries, and blueberries.

Spoon equally into the mugs and bake for 25 to 30 minutes, or until puffed and slightly cracked on top. Remove from oven and cool 15 minutes.

Sprinkle with powdered sugar just before serving. Serve warm with whipped cream or vanilla ice cream.

Green Living Tip

Reuse! Use glass containers, cups, mugs, and bowls in different ways than their original use.

No-Bake Brownie Cupcakes

Ingredients

- 1 package brownie mix
- ⅔ cup milk
- ½ cup butter
- 1 cup peanut butter
- 1 teaspoon vanilla
- 3 cups quick-cooking oats
- 1 cup candy-coated chocolate pieces

Garnish

- 1 cup whipped cream
- ½ cup candy-coated chocolate pieces

Makes 2 dozen

Line muffin cups with silicone or paper muffin liners. Place muffin pans on a sheet pan. Spray liners with nonstick cooking spray and set aside.

In large saucepan, combine brownie mix, milk, and butter. Cook over medium heat until mixture comes to a boil, stirring occasionally. Boil 1 to 2 minutes, stirring constantly. Carefully remove from heat.

Whisk in peanut butter and vanilla until well combined. Stir in oats 1 cup at a time. Fold in chocolate pieces.

Spoon batter equally into each muffin cup and place in refrigerator for 2 hours before serving. Garnish with whipped cream and additional candy-coated pieces.

Green Living Tip

You can make this no-bake dessert without using gas or electricity from the oven at all! It also keeps the house cooler in the summertime if you don't use the oven. That way you're not tempted to turn up the air-conditioning and use even more electricity!

Strawberry Chopstick Pops

Ingredients

● ● ● ● ● ● ● ●

1 pint vanilla yogurt

12 fresh organic strawberries (remove stems only not core)

6 bamboo chopsticks

Assorted Toppings

½ cup chopped assorted nuts

½ cup shredded coconut

¼ cup confetti sprinkles

Makes 6

Line a sheet pan with Silpat or a clean brown paper grocery bag cut to fit. Set aside.

Spoon 1 cup yogurt into a small mug or bowl. Insert 1 bamboo chopstick into the stem end of 2 strawberries.

Using the chopstick as a skewer, dip the strawberry pops into the yogurt. Repeat for remaining strawberries and chopsticks. Add yogurt to mug or bowl as needed.

Lay each pop on the prepared sheet pan and decorate with nuts, coconut, and sprinkles. Place in freezer for at least 2 hours before covering or serving. Store covered in freezer until ready to serve.

Green Cuisine Tip

Bamboo regrows faster and more easily than hardwood and harvesting it has less of a negative impact on the environment. Use eco-friendly bamboo chopsticks. You can also use bamboo kitchen utensils. Use real plates and glasses and cloth napkins (which can be washed and used over and over) instead of paper plates, plastic cups, and paper napkins that are thrown away after using.

All You Need Is Love Cookies

Ingredients

Cookies

1 cup unsalted butter, softened

1½ cups sugar

2 eggs

3 teaspoons vanilla

2¾ cups whole-wheat pastry flour

¼ teaspoon salt

Food coloring

Powdered sugar for rolling out dough

Glaze

2 cups powdered sugar

3 tablespoons milk

½ teaspoon vanilla

Food coloring

Makes 24–30

Cream the butter and sugar in a large mixing bowl. Beat in the eggs one at a time. Stir in the vanilla.

Combine the flour and salt in another small bowl, and then stir into the butter mixture until well combined.

Divide dough into 3 to 4 equal portions and add a different color food dye to each one. Work color into each dough section to swirl colors throughout. Combine all different colored dough portions into one ball and flatten into a disc. Cover and quick-chill in freezer 1½ hours.

Preheat oven to 350 degrees F. Line 2 cookie sheets with Silpat, unbleached parchment paper, or a clean brown paper grocery bag cut to fit.

Lightly dust work area with powdered sugar. Remove dough from freezer in small portions and roll out to ¼ inch thickness. Cut out with a heart-shaped cookie cutter and place 1 inch apart on prepared cookie sheets. Bake 8 to 10 minutes or until barely golden.

In a medium size bowl, stir together powdered sugar, half of the milk, and vanilla. Divide glaze between 3 small bowls and add a different color to each bowl. Add more milk to make a slightly runny consistency if needed.

Spoon different colored glazes on top of each cookie and let them all run together to form a swirl of colors. Allow the glaze to dry completely before removing cookies to an airtight container for storage.

Collect them all!

www.gibbs-smith.com

www.batterupkids.com

www.kidscookingshop.com